Incident Report Log Book

COMPANY DETAILS

COMPANY

ADDRESS

E-MAIL ADDRESS

WEBSITE

PHONE FAX

EMERGENCY CONTACT PERSON

PHONE FAX

LOG BOOK DETAILS

CONTINUED FROM LOG BOOK

LOG START DATE

CONTINUED TO LOG BOOK

LOG END DATE

Incident Report Log Book

INCIDENT REPORT FORM

INCIDENT DATE

REPORT DATE

INCIDENT TIME

LOCATION

PERSON INVOLVED / INJURED ☐ **EMPLOYEE** ☐ **VISITOR** ☐ **OTHER / ....**

FULL NAME

ADDRESS

PHONE NUMBER

E-MAIL

DESCRIPTION OF INCIDENT

....
....
....
....
....
....

ACTION TAKEN

....
....
....
....

WITNESS/ES

FULL NAME

CONTACT

FULL NAME

CONTACT

FULL NAME

CONTACT

FORM COMPLETED BY

SIGNED BY

APPROVED BY

SIGNED BY

Incident Report Log Book

INCIDENT REPORT FORM

INCIDENT DATE		**REPORT DATE**	
INCIDENT TIME		**LOCATION**	

PERSON INVOLVED / INJURED ☐ EMPLOYEE ☐ VISITOR ☐ OTHER / ....

FULL NAME

ADDRESS

PHONE NUMBER   **E-MAIL**

DESCRIPTION OF INCIDENT

....
....
....
....
....
....

ACTION TAKEN

....
....
....
....

WITNESS/ES

FULL NAME		**CONTACT**
FULL NAME		**CONTACT**
FULL NAME		**CONTACT**
FORM COMPLETED BY		**SIGNED BY**
APPROVED BY		**SIGNED BY**

Incident Report Log Book

INCIDENT REPORT FORM

INCIDENT DATE .... REPORT DATE ....

INCIDENT TIME .... LOCATION ....

PERSON INVOLVED / INJURED ☐ EMPLOYEE ☐ VISITOR ☐ OTHER / ....

FULL NAME ....

ADDRESS ....

PHONE NUMBER .... E-MAIL ....

DESCRIPTION OF INCIDENT

....
....
....
....
....
....

ACTION TAKEN

....
....
....
....

WITNESS/ES

FULL NAME .... CONTACT ....

FULL NAME .... CONTACT ....

FULL NAME .... CONTACT ....

FORM COMPLETED BY .... SIGNED BY ....

APPROVED BY .... SIGNED BY ....

Incident Report Log Book

INCIDENT REPORT FORM

INCIDENT DATE   REPORT DATE

INCIDENT TIME   LOCATION

PERSON INVOLVED / INJURED   ☐ EMPLOYEE   ☐ VISITOR   ☐ OTHER / ....

FULL NAME

ADDRESS

PHONE NUMBER   E-MAIL

DESCRIPTION OF INCIDENT

....
....
....
....
....
....

ACTION TAKEN

....
....
....
....

WITNESS/ES

FULL NAME   CONTACT

FULL NAME   CONTACT

FULL NAME   CONTACT

FORM COMPLETED BY   SIGNED BY

APPROVED BY   SIGNED BY

Incident Report Log Book

INCIDENT REPORT FORM

INCIDENT DATE

REPORT DATE

INCIDENT TIME

LOCATION

PERSON INVOLVED / INJURED ☐ EMPLOYEE ☐ VISITOR ☐ OTHER / ....

FULL NAME

ADDRESS

PHONE NUMBER

E-MAIL

DESCRIPTION OF INCIDENT

....
....
....
....
....
....

ACTION TAKEN

....
....
....
....

WITNESS/ES

FULL NAME

CONTACT

FULL NAME

CONTACT

FULL NAME

CONTACT

FORM COMPLETED BY

SIGNED BY

APPROVED BY

SIGNED BY

Incident Report Log Book

INCIDENT REPORT FORM

INCIDENT DATE .... **REPORT DATE** ....

INCIDENT TIME .... **LOCATION** ....

PERSON INVOLVED / INJURED ☐ EMPLOYEE ☐ VISITOR ☐ OTHER / ....

FULL NAME ....

ADDRESS ....

PHONE NUMBER .... **E-MAIL** ....

DESCRIPTION OF INCIDENT

....
....
....
....
....
....

ACTION TAKEN

....
....
....
....

WITNESS/ES

FULL NAME .... **CONTACT** ....

FULL NAME .... **CONTACT** ....

FULL NAME .... **CONTACT** ....

FORM COMPLETED BY .... **SIGNED BY** ....

APPROVED BY .... **SIGNED BY** ....

Incident Report Log Book

INCIDENT REPORT FORM

INCIDENT DATE   REPORT DATE

INCIDENT TIME   LOCATION

PERSON INVOLVED / INJURED   ☐ EMPLOYEE   ☐ VISITOR   ☐ OTHER / ....

FULL NAME

ADDRESS

PHONE NUMBER   E-MAIL

DESCRIPTION OF INCIDENT

....
....
....
....
....
....

ACTION TAKEN

....
....
....
....

WITNESS/ES

FULL NAME   CONTACT

FULL NAME   CONTACT

FULL NAME   CONTACT

FORM COMPLETED BY   SIGNED BY

APPROVED BY   SIGNED BY

Incident Report Log Book

INCIDENT REPORT FORM

INCIDENT DATE

REPORT DATE

INCIDENT TIME

LOCATION

PERSON INVOLVED / INJURED   ☐ EMPLOYEE   ☐ VISITOR   ☐ OTHER / ....

FULL NAME

ADDRESS

PHONE NUMBER   E-MAIL

DESCRIPTION OF INCIDENT

....
....
....
....
....
....

ACTION TAKEN

....
....
....
....

WITNESS/ES

FULL NAME   CONTACT

FULL NAME   CONTACT

FULL NAME   CONTACT

FORM COMPLETED BY   SIGNED BY

APPROVED BY   SIGNED BY

Incident Report Log Book

INCIDENT REPORT FORM

INCIDENT DATE

REPORT DATE

INCIDENT TIME

LOCATION

PERSON INVOLVED / INJURED ☐ EMPLOYEE ☐ VISITOR ☐ OTHER / ....

FULL NAME

ADDRESS

PHONE NUMBER   E-MAIL

DESCRIPTION OF INCIDENT

....
....
....
....
....
....

ACTION TAKEN

....
....
....
....

WITNESS/ES

FULL NAME   CONTACT

FULL NAME   CONTACT

FULL NAME   CONTACT

FORM COMPLETED BY   SIGNED BY

APPROVED BY   SIGNED BY

Incident Report Log Book

INCIDENT REPORT FORM

INCIDENT DATE

REPORT DATE

INCIDENT TIME

LOCATION

PERSON INVOLVED / INJURED ☐ EMPLOYEE ☐ VISITOR ☐ OTHER / ....

FULL NAME

ADDRESS

PHONE NUMBER

E-MAIL

DESCRIPTION OF INCIDENT

....
....
....
....
....
....

ACTION TAKEN

....
....
....
....

WITNESS/ES

FULL NAME

CONTACT

FULL NAME

CONTACT

FULL NAME

CONTACT

FORM COMPLETED BY

SIGNED BY

APPROVED BY

SIGNED BY

Incident Report Log Book

INCIDENT REPORT FORM

INCIDENT DATE

REPORT DATE

INCIDENT TIME

LOCATION

PERSON INVOLVED / INJURED   ☐ EMPLOYEE   ☐ VISITOR   ☐ OTHER / ....

FULL NAME

ADDRESS

PHONE NUMBER   E-MAIL

DESCRIPTION OF INCIDENT

....
....
....
....
....
....

ACTION TAKEN

....
....
....
....

WITNESS/ES

FULL NAME   CONTACT

FULL NAME   CONTACT

FULL NAME   CONTACT

FORM COMPLETED BY   SIGNED BY

APPROVED BY   SIGNED BY

Incident Report Log Book

INCIDENT REPORT FORM

INCIDENT DATE

REPORT DATE

INCIDENT TIME

LOCATION

PERSON INVOLVED / INJURED
☐ EMPLOYEE   ☐ VISITOR   ☐ OTHER / ....

FULL NAME

ADDRESS

PHONE NUMBER   E-MAIL

DESCRIPTION OF INCIDENT

....
....
....
....
....
....

ACTION TAKEN

....
....
....
....

WITNESS/ES

FULL NAME   CONTACT

FULL NAME   CONTACT

FULL NAME   CONTACT

FORM COMPLETED BY   SIGNED BY

APPROVED BY   SIGNED BY

Incident Report Log Book

INCIDENT REPORT FORM

INCIDENT DATE

REPORT DATE

INCIDENT TIME

LOCATION

PERSON INVOLVED / INJURED   ☐ **EMPLOYEE**   ☐ **VISITOR**   ☐ **OTHER /** ....

FULL NAME

ADDRESS

PHONE NUMBER

E-MAIL

DESCRIPTION OF INCIDENT

....
....
....
....
....
....

ACTION TAKEN

....
....
....
....

WITNESS/ES

FULL NAME

CONTACT

FULL NAME

CONTACT

FULL NAME

CONTACT

FORM COMPLETED BY

SIGNED BY

APPROVED BY

SIGNED BY

Incident Report Log Book

INCIDENT REPORT FORM

INCIDENT DATE

REPORT DATE

INCIDENT TIME

LOCATION

PERSON INVOLVED / INJURED ☐ EMPLOYEE ☐ VISITOR ☐ OTHER / ....

FULL NAME

ADDRESS

PHONE NUMBER

E-MAIL

DESCRIPTION OF INCIDENT

....
....
....
....
....
....

ACTION TAKEN

....
....
....
....

WITNESS/ES

FULL NAME

CONTACT

FULL NAME

CONTACT

FULL NAME

CONTACT

FORM COMPLETED BY

SIGNED BY

APPROVED BY

SIGNED BY

Incident Report Log Book

INCIDENT REPORT FORM

INCIDENT DATE _____ **REPORT DATE** _____

INCIDENT TIME _____ **LOCATION** _____

PERSON INVOLVED / INJURED ☐ EMPLOYEE ☐ VISITOR ☐ OTHER / ....

FULL NAME _____

ADDRESS _____

PHONE NUMBER _____ **E-MAIL** _____

DESCRIPTION OF INCIDENT

....
....
....
....
....
....

ACTION TAKEN

....
....
....
....

WITNESS/ES

FULL NAME _____ **CONTACT** _____

FULL NAME _____ **CONTACT** _____

FULL NAME _____ **CONTACT** _____

FORM COMPLETED BY _____ **SIGNED BY** _____

APPROVED BY _____ **SIGNED BY** _____

Incident Report Log Book

INCIDENT REPORT FORM

INCIDENT DATE

REPORT DATE

INCIDENT TIME

LOCATION

PERSON INVOLVED / INJURED ☐ EMPLOYEE ☐ VISITOR ☐ OTHER / ....

FULL NAME

ADDRESS

PHONE NUMBER   E-MAIL

DESCRIPTION OF INCIDENT

....
....
....
....
....
....

ACTION TAKEN

....
....
....
....

WITNESS/ES

FULL NAME   CONTACT

FULL NAME   CONTACT

FULL NAME   CONTACT

FORM COMPLETED BY   SIGNED BY

APPROVED BY   SIGNED BY

Incident Report Log Book

INCIDENT REPORT FORM

INCIDENT DATE   REPORT DATE

INCIDENT TIME   LOCATION

PERSON INVOLVED / INJURED   ☐ EMPLOYEE   ☐ VISITOR   ☐ OTHER / ....

FULL NAME

ADDRESS

PHONE NUMBER   E-MAIL

DESCRIPTION OF INCIDENT

....
....
....
....
....
....

ACTION TAKEN

....
....
....
....

WITNESS/ES

FULL NAME   CONTACT

FULL NAME   CONTACT

FULL NAME   CONTACT

FORM COMPLETED BY   SIGNED BY

APPROVED BY   SIGNED BY

Incident Report Log Book

INCIDENT REPORT FORM

INCIDENT DATE	**REPORT DATE**
INCIDENT TIME	**LOCATION**

PERSON INVOLVED / INJURED ☐ EMPLOYEE ☐ VISITOR ☐ OTHER / ....

FULL NAME

ADDRESS

PHONE NUMBER **E-MAIL**

DESCRIPTION OF INCIDENT

....
....
....
....
....
....

ACTION TAKEN

....
....
....
....

WITNESS/ES

FULL NAME	**CONTACT**
FULL NAME	**CONTACT**
FULL NAME	**CONTACT**
FORM COMPLETED BY	**SIGNED BY**
APPROVED BY	**SIGNED BY**

Incident Report Log Book

INCIDENT REPORT FORM

INCIDENT DATE

REPORT DATE

INCIDENT TIME

LOCATION

PERSON INVOLVED / INJURED ☐ EMPLOYEE ☐ VISITOR ☐ OTHER / ....

FULL NAME

ADDRESS

PHONE NUMBER

E-MAIL

DESCRIPTION OF INCIDENT

....
....
....
....
....
....

ACTION TAKEN

....
....
....
....

WITNESS/ES

FULL NAME

CONTACT

FULL NAME

CONTACT

FULL NAME

CONTACT

FORM COMPLETED BY

SIGNED BY

APPROVED BY

SIGNED BY

Incident Report Log Book

INCIDENT REPORT FORM

INCIDENT DATE

REPORT DATE

INCIDENT TIME

LOCATION

PERSON INVOLVED / INJURED ☐ EMPLOYEE ☐ VISITOR ☐ OTHER / ....

FULL NAME

ADDRESS

PHONE NUMBER

E-MAIL

DESCRIPTION OF INCIDENT

....
....
....
....
....
....

ACTION TAKEN

....
....
....
....

WITNESS/ES

FULL NAME

CONTACT

FULL NAME

CONTACT

FULL NAME

CONTACT

FORM COMPLETED BY

SIGNED BY

APPROVED BY

SIGNED BY

Incident Report Log Book

INCIDENT REPORT FORM

INCIDENT DATE		**REPORT DATE**	
INCIDENT TIME		**LOCATION**	

PERSON INVOLVED / INJURED ☐ **EMPLOYEE** ☐ **VISITOR** ☐ **OTHER / ....**

FULL NAME

ADDRESS

PHONE NUMBER   **E-MAIL**

DESCRIPTION OF INCIDENT

....
....
....
....
....
....

ACTION TAKEN

....
....
....
....

WITNESS/ES

FULL NAME		**CONTACT**	
FULL NAME		**CONTACT**	
FULL NAME		**CONTACT**	
FORM COMPLETED BY		**SIGNED BY**	
APPROVED BY		**SIGNED BY**	

Incident Report Log Book

INCIDENT REPORT FORM

INCIDENT DATE _____ REPORT DATE _____

INCIDENT TIME _____ LOCATION _____

PERSON INVOLVED / INJURED ☐ EMPLOYEE ☐ VISITOR ☐ OTHER / ....

FULL NAME _____

ADDRESS _____

PHONE NUMBER _____ E-MAIL

DESCRIPTION OF INCIDENT

....
....
....
....
....
....

ACTION TAKEN

....
....
....
....

WITNESS/ES

FULL NAME _____ CONTACT _____

FULL NAME _____ CONTACT _____

FULL NAME _____ CONTACT _____

FORM COMPLETED BY _____ SIGNED BY _____

APPROVED BY _____ SIGNED BY _____

Incident Report Log Book

INCIDENT REPORT FORM

INCIDENT DATE _____   REPORT DATE _____

INCIDENT TIME _____   LOCATION _____

PERSON INVOLVED / INJURED   ☐ EMPLOYEE   ☐ VISITOR   ☐ OTHER / ....

FULL NAME _____

ADDRESS _____

PHONE NUMBER _____   E-MAIL _____

DESCRIPTION OF INCIDENT

....
....
....
....
....
....

ACTION TAKEN

....
....
....
....

WITNESS/ES

FULL NAME _____   CONTACT _____

FULL NAME _____   CONTACT _____

FULL NAME _____   CONTACT _____

FORM COMPLETED BY _____   SIGNED BY _____

APPROVED BY _____   SIGNED BY _____

Incident Report Log Book

INCIDENT REPORT FORM

INCIDENT DATE

REPORT DATE

INCIDENT TIME

LOCATION

PERSON INVOLVED / INJURED ☐ EMPLOYEE ☐ VISITOR ☐ OTHER / ....

FULL NAME

ADDRESS

PHONE NUMBER

E-MAIL

DESCRIPTION OF INCIDENT

....
....
....
....
....
....

ACTION TAKEN

....
....
....
....

WITNESS/ES

FULL NAME

CONTACT

FULL NAME

CONTACT

FULL NAME

CONTACT

FORM COMPLETED BY

SIGNED BY

APPROVED BY

SIGNED BY

Incident Report Log Book

INCIDENT REPORT FORM

INCIDENT DATE

REPORT DATE

INCIDENT TIME

LOCATION

PERSON INVOLVED / INJURED ☐ **EMPLOYEE** ☐ **VISITOR** ☐ **OTHER /** ....

FULL NAME

ADDRESS

PHONE NUMBER

E-MAIL

DESCRIPTION OF INCIDENT

....
....
....
....
....
....

ACTION TAKEN

....
....
....
....

WITNESS/ES

FULL NAME

CONTACT

FULL NAME

CONTACT

FULL NAME

CONTACT

FORM COMPLETED BY

SIGNED BY

APPROVED BY

SIGNED BY

Incident Report Log Book

INCIDENT REPORT FORM

INCIDENT DATE

REPORT DATE

INCIDENT TIME

LOCATION

PERSON INVOLVED / INJURED   ☐ EMPLOYEE   ☐ VISITOR   ☐ OTHER / ....

FULL NAME

ADDRESS

PHONE NUMBER   E-MAIL

DESCRIPTION OF INCIDENT

....
....
....
....
....
....

ACTION TAKEN

....
....
....
....

WITNESS/ES

FULL NAME   CONTACT

FULL NAME   CONTACT

FULL NAME   CONTACT

FORM COMPLETED BY   SIGNED BY

APPROVED BY   SIGNED BY

Incident Report Log Book

INCIDENT REPORT FORM

INCIDENT DATE   **REPORT DATE**

INCIDENT TIME   **LOCATION**

PERSON INVOLVED / INJURED   ☐ **EMPLOYEE**   ☐ **VISITOR**   ☐ **OTHER /** ....

FULL NAME

ADDRESS

PHONE NUMBER   **E-MAIL**

DESCRIPTION OF INCIDENT

....
....
....
....
....
....

ACTION TAKEN

....
....
....
....

WITNESS/ES

FULL NAME   **CONTACT**

FULL NAME   **CONTACT**

FULL NAME   **CONTACT**

FORM COMPLETED BY   **SIGNED BY**

APPROVED BY   **SIGNED BY**

Incident Report Log Book

INCIDENT REPORT FORM

INCIDENT DATE   **REPORT DATE**

INCIDENT TIME   **LOCATION**

PERSON INVOLVED / INJURED   ☐ EMPLOYEE   ☐ VISITOR   ☐ OTHER / ....

FULL NAME

ADDRESS

PHONE NUMBER   **E-MAIL**

DESCRIPTION OF INCIDENT

....
....
....
....
....
....

ACTION TAKEN

....
....
....
....

WITNESS/ES

FULL NAME   **CONTACT**

FULL NAME   **CONTACT**

FULL NAME   **CONTACT**

FORM COMPLETED BY   **SIGNED BY**

APPROVED BY   **SIGNED BY**

Incident Report Log Book

INCIDENT REPORT FORM

INCIDENT DATE

REPORT DATE

INCIDENT TIME

LOCATION

PERSON INVOLVED / INJURED ☐ EMPLOYEE ☐ VISITOR ☐ OTHER / ....

FULL NAME

ADDRESS

PHONE NUMBER E-MAIL

DESCRIPTION OF INCIDENT

....
....
....
....
....
....

ACTION TAKEN

....
....
....
....

WITNESS/ES

FULL NAME CONTACT

FULL NAME CONTACT

FULL NAME CONTACT

FORM COMPLETED BY SIGNED BY

APPROVED BY SIGNED BY

Incident Report Log Book

INCIDENT REPORT FORM

INCIDENT DATE

REPORT DATE

INCIDENT TIME

LOCATION

PERSON INVOLVED / INJURED ☐ EMPLOYEE ☐ VISITOR ☐ OTHER / ....

FULL NAME

ADDRESS

PHONE NUMBER   E-MAIL

DESCRIPTION OF INCIDENT

....
....
....
....
....
....

ACTION TAKEN

....
....
....
....

WITNESS/ES

FULL NAME   CONTACT

FULL NAME   CONTACT

FULL NAME   CONTACT

FORM COMPLETED BY   SIGNED BY

APPROVED BY   SIGNED BY

Incident Report Log Book

INCIDENT REPORT FORM

INCIDENT DATE   REPORT DATE

INCIDENT TIME   LOCATION

PERSON INVOLVED / INJURED   ☐ EMPLOYEE   ☐ VISITOR   ☐ OTHER / ....

FULL NAME

ADDRESS

PHONE NUMBER   E-MAIL

DESCRIPTION OF INCIDENT

....
....
....
....
....
....

ACTION TAKEN

....
....
....
....

WITNESS/ES

FULL NAME   CONTACT

FULL NAME   CONTACT

FULL NAME   CONTACT

FORM COMPLETED BY   SIGNED BY

APPROVED BY   SIGNED BY

Incident Report Log Book

INCIDENT REPORT FORM

INCIDENT DATE

REPORT DATE

INCIDENT TIME

LOCATION

PERSON INVOLVED / INJURED ☐ EMPLOYEE ☐ VISITOR ☐ OTHER / ....

FULL NAME

ADDRESS

PHONE NUMBER

E-MAIL

DESCRIPTION OF INCIDENT

....
....
....
....
....
....

ACTION TAKEN

....
....
....
....

WITNESS/ES

FULL NAME

CONTACT

FULL NAME

CONTACT

FULL NAME

CONTACT

FORM COMPLETED BY

SIGNED BY

APPROVED BY

SIGNED BY

Incident Report Log Book

INCIDENT REPORT FORM

INCIDENT DATE _____   REPORT DATE _____

INCIDENT TIME _____   LOCATION _____

PERSON INVOLVED / INJURED   ☐ EMPLOYEE   ☐ VISITOR   ☐ OTHER / ....

FULL NAME _____

ADDRESS _____

PHONE NUMBER _____   E-MAIL _____

DESCRIPTION OF INCIDENT

....
....
....
....
....
....

ACTION TAKEN

....
....
....
....

WITNESS/ES

FULL NAME _____   CONTACT _____

FULL NAME _____   CONTACT _____

FULL NAME _____   CONTACT _____

FORM COMPLETED BY _____   SIGNED BY _____

APPROVED BY _____   SIGNED BY _____

Incident Report Log Book

INCIDENT REPORT FORM

INCIDENT DATE		**REPORT DATE**
INCIDENT TIME		**LOCATION**

PERSON INVOLVED / INJURED ☐ **EMPLOYEE** ☐ **VISITOR** ☐ **OTHER /** ....

FULL NAME

ADDRESS

PHONE NUMBER   **E-MAIL**

DESCRIPTION OF INCIDENT

....
....
....
....
....
....

ACTION TAKEN

....
....
....
....

WITNESS/ES

FULL NAME	**CONTACT**
FULL NAME	**CONTACT**
FULL NAME	**CONTACT**
FORM COMPLETED BY	**SIGNED BY**
APPROVED BY	**SIGNED BY**

Incident Report Log Book

INCIDENT REPORT FORM

INCIDENT DATE	**REPORT DATE**
INCIDENT TIME	**LOCATION**

PERSON INVOLVED / INJURED ☐ **EMPLOYEE** ☐ **VISITOR** ☐ **OTHER /** ....

FULL NAME

ADDRESS

PHONE NUMBER   **E-MAIL**

DESCRIPTION OF INCIDENT

....
....
....
....
....
....

ACTION TAKEN

....
....
....
....

WITNESS/ES

FULL NAME	**CONTACT**
FULL NAME	**CONTACT**
FULL NAME	**CONTACT**
FORM COMPLETED BY	**SIGNED BY**
APPROVED BY	**SIGNED BY**

Incident Report Log Book

INCIDENT REPORT FORM

INCIDENT DATE

REPORT DATE

INCIDENT TIME

LOCATION

PERSON INVOLVED / INJURED ☐ EMPLOYEE ☐ VISITOR ☐ OTHER / ....

FULL NAME

ADDRESS

PHONE NUMBER

E-MAIL

DESCRIPTION OF INCIDENT

....
....
....
....
....
....

ACTION TAKEN

....
....
....
....

WITNESS/ES

FULL NAME

CONTACT

FULL NAME

CONTACT

FULL NAME

CONTACT

FORM COMPLETED BY

SIGNED BY

APPROVED BY

SIGNED BY

Incident Report Log Book

INCIDENT REPORT FORM

INCIDENT DATE		**REPORT DATE**	
INCIDENT TIME		**LOCATION**	

PERSON INVOLVED / INJURED ☐ **EMPLOYEE** ☐ **VISITOR** ☐ **OTHER** / ....

FULL NAME

ADDRESS

PHONE NUMBER   **E-MAIL**

DESCRIPTION OF INCIDENT

....
....
....
....
....
....

ACTION TAKEN

....
....
....
....

WITNESS/ES

FULL NAME	**CONTACT**	
FULL NAME	**CONTACT**	
FULL NAME	**CONTACT**	
FORM COMPLETED BY	**SIGNED BY**	
APPROVED BY	**SIGNED BY**	

Incident Report Log Book

INCIDENT REPORT FORM

INCIDENT DATE

REPORT DATE

INCIDENT TIME

LOCATION

PERSON INVOLVED / INJURED ☐ EMPLOYEE ☐ VISITOR ☐ OTHER / ....

FULL NAME

ADDRESS

PHONE NUMBER

E-MAIL

DESCRIPTION OF INCIDENT

....
....
....
....
....
....

ACTION TAKEN

....
....
....
....

WITNESS/ES

FULL NAME

CONTACT

FULL NAME

CONTACT

FULL NAME

CONTACT

FORM COMPLETED BY

SIGNED BY

APPROVED BY

SIGNED BY

Incident Report Log Book

INCIDENT REPORT FORM

INCIDENT DATE

REPORT DATE

INCIDENT TIME

LOCATION

PERSON INVOLVED / INJURED ☐ EMPLOYEE ☐ VISITOR ☐ OTHER / ....

FULL NAME

ADDRESS

PHONE NUMBER

E-MAIL

DESCRIPTION OF INCIDENT

....
....
....
....
....
....

ACTION TAKEN

....
....
....
....

WITNESS/ES

FULL NAME

CONTACT

FULL NAME

CONTACT

FULL NAME

CONTACT

FORM COMPLETED BY

SIGNED BY

APPROVED BY

SIGNED BY

Incident Report Log Book

INCIDENT REPORT FORM

INCIDENT DATE   **REPORT DATE**

INCIDENT TIME   **LOCATION**

PERSON INVOLVED / INJURED   ☐ **EMPLOYEE**   ☐ **VISITOR**   ☐ **OTHER /** ....

FULL NAME

ADDRESS

PHONE NUMBER   **E-MAIL**

DESCRIPTION OF INCIDENT

....
....
....
....
....
....

ACTION TAKEN

....
....
....
....

WITNESS/ES

FULL NAME   **CONTACT**

FULL NAME   **CONTACT**

FULL NAME   **CONTACT**

FORM COMPLETED BY   **SIGNED BY**

APPROVED BY   **SIGNED BY**

Incident Report Log Book

INCIDENT REPORT FORM

INCIDENT DATE	**REPORT DATE**
INCIDENT TIME	**LOCATION**

PERSON INVOLVED / INJURED ☐ **EMPLOYEE** ☐ **VISITOR** ☐ **OTHER /** ....

FULL NAME

ADDRESS

PHONE NUMBER	**E-MAIL**

DESCRIPTION OF INCIDENT

....
....
....
....
....
....

ACTION TAKEN

....
....
....
....

WITNESS/ES

FULL NAME	**CONTACT**
FULL NAME	**CONTACT**
FULL NAME	**CONTACT**
FORM COMPLETED BY	**SIGNED BY**
APPROVED BY	**SIGNED BY**

Incident Report Log Book

INCIDENT REPORT FORM

INCIDENT DATE _____   REPORT DATE _____

INCIDENT TIME _____   LOCATION _____

PERSON INVOLVED / INJURED   ☐ EMPLOYEE   ☐ VISITOR   ☐ OTHER / ....

FULL NAME _____

ADDRESS _____

PHONE NUMBER _____   E-MAIL _____

DESCRIPTION OF INCIDENT

....
....
....
....
....
....

ACTION TAKEN

....
....
....
....

WITNESS/ES

FULL NAME _____   CONTACT _____

FULL NAME _____   CONTACT _____

FULL NAME _____   CONTACT _____

FORM COMPLETED BY _____   SIGNED BY _____

APPROVED BY _____   SIGNED BY _____

Incident Report Log Book

INCIDENT REPORT FORM

INCIDENT DATE

REPORT DATE

INCIDENT TIME

LOCATION

PERSON INVOLVED / INJURED   ☐ EMPLOYEE   ☐ VISITOR   ☐ OTHER / ....

FULL NAME

ADDRESS

PHONE NUMBER

E-MAIL

DESCRIPTION OF INCIDENT

....
....
....
....
....
....

ACTION TAKEN

....
....
....
....

WITNESS/ES

FULL NAME

CONTACT

FULL NAME

CONTACT

FULL NAME

CONTACT

FORM COMPLETED BY

SIGNED BY

APPROVED BY

SIGNED BY

Incident Report Log Book

INCIDENT REPORT FORM

INCIDENT DATE

REPORT DATE

INCIDENT TIME

LOCATION

PERSON INVOLVED / INJURED ☐ EMPLOYEE ☐ VISITOR ☐ OTHER / ....

FULL NAME

ADDRESS

PHONE NUMBER

E-MAIL

DESCRIPTION OF INCIDENT

....

....

....

....

....

....

ACTION TAKEN

....

....

....

....

WITNESS/ES

FULL NAME

CONTACT

FULL NAME

CONTACT

FULL NAME

CONTACT

FORM COMPLETED BY

SIGNED BY

APPROVED BY

SIGNED BY

Incident Report Log Book

INCIDENT REPORT FORM

INCIDENT DATE   **REPORT DATE**

INCIDENT TIME   **LOCATION**

PERSON INVOLVED / INJURED   ☐ **EMPLOYEE**   ☐ **VISITOR**   ☐ **OTHER /** ....

FULL NAME

ADDRESS

PHONE NUMBER   **E-MAIL**

DESCRIPTION OF INCIDENT

....
....
....
....
....
....

ACTION TAKEN

....
....
....
....

WITNESS/ES

FULL NAME   **CONTACT**

FULL NAME   **CONTACT**

FULL NAME   **CONTACT**

FORM COMPLETED BY   **SIGNED BY**

APPROVED BY   **SIGNED BY**

Incident Report Log Book

INCIDENT REPORT FORM

INCIDENT DATE _____   REPORT DATE _____

INCIDENT TIME _____   LOCATION _____

PERSON INVOLVED / INJURED ☐ EMPLOYEE ☐ VISITOR ☐ OTHER / ....

FULL NAME _____

ADDRESS _____

PHONE NUMBER _____   E-MAIL _____

DESCRIPTION OF INCIDENT

....
....
....
....
....
....

ACTION TAKEN

....
....
....
....

WITNESS/ES

FULL NAME _____   CONTACT _____

FULL NAME _____   CONTACT _____

FULL NAME _____   CONTACT _____

FORM COMPLETED BY _____   SIGNED BY _____

APPROVED BY _____   SIGNED BY _____

Incident Report Log Book

INCIDENT REPORT FORM

INCIDENT DATE

REPORT DATE

INCIDENT TIME

LOCATION

PERSON INVOLVED / INJURED ☐ **EMPLOYEE** ☐ **VISITOR** ☐ **OTHER / ....**

FULL NAME

ADDRESS

PHONE NUMBER **E-MAIL**

DESCRIPTION OF INCIDENT

....
....
....
....
....
....

ACTION TAKEN

....
....
....
....

WITNESS/ES

FULL NAME **CONTACT**

FULL NAME **CONTACT**

FULL NAME **CONTACT**

FORM COMPLETED BY **SIGNED BY**

APPROVED BY **SIGNED BY**

Incident Report Log Book

INCIDENT REPORT FORM

INCIDENT DATE .... REPORT DATE ....

INCIDENT TIME .... LOCATION ....

PERSON INVOLVED / INJURED ☐ EMPLOYEE ☐ VISITOR ☐ OTHER / ....

FULL NAME ....

ADDRESS ....

PHONE NUMBER .... E-MAIL ....

DESCRIPTION OF INCIDENT

....
....
....
....
....
....

ACTION TAKEN

....
....
....
....

WITNESS/ES

FULL NAME .... CONTACT ....

FULL NAME .... CONTACT ....

FULL NAME .... CONTACT ....

FORM COMPLETED BY .... SIGNED BY ....

APPROVED BY .... SIGNED BY ....

Incident Report Log Book

INCIDENT REPORT FORM

INCIDENT DATE

INCIDENT TIME

REPORT DATE

LOCATION

PERSON INVOLVED / INJURED ☐ **EMPLOYEE** ☐ **VISITOR** ☐ **OTHER /** ....

FULL NAME

ADDRESS

PHONE NUMBER   **E-MAIL**

DESCRIPTION OF INCIDENT

....
....
....
....
....
....

ACTION TAKEN

....
....
....
....

WITNESS/ES

FULL NAME   **CONTACT**

FULL NAME   **CONTACT**

FULL NAME   **CONTACT**

FORM COMPLETED BY   **SIGNED BY**

APPROVED BY   **SIGNED BY**

Incident Report Log Book

INCIDENT REPORT FORM

INCIDENT DATE

REPORT DATE

INCIDENT TIME

LOCATION

PERSON INVOLVED / INJURED ☐ EMPLOYEE ☐ VISITOR ☐ OTHER / ....

FULL NAME

ADDRESS

PHONE NUMBER

E-MAIL

DESCRIPTION OF INCIDENT

....
....
....
....
....
....

ACTION TAKEN

....
....
....
....

WITNESS/ES

FULL NAME

CONTACT

FULL NAME

CONTACT

FULL NAME

CONTACT

FORM COMPLETED BY

SIGNED BY

APPROVED BY

SIGNED BY

Incident Report Log Book

INCIDENT REPORT FORM

INCIDENT DATE		**REPORT DATE**	
INCIDENT TIME		**LOCATION**	

PERSON INVOLVED / INJURED ☐ **EMPLOYEE** ☐ **VISITOR** ☐ **OTHER /** ....

FULL NAME

ADDRESS

PHONE NUMBER　　　　　　　　　**E-MAIL**

DESCRIPTION OF INCIDENT

....
....
....
....
....
....

ACTION TAKEN

....
....
....
....

WITNESS/ES

FULL NAME		**CONTACT**
FULL NAME		**CONTACT**
FULL NAME		**CONTACT**
FORM COMPLETED BY		**SIGNED BY**
APPROVED BY		**SIGNED BY**

Incident Report Log Book

INCIDENT REPORT FORM

INCIDENT DATE

REPORT DATE

INCIDENT TIME

LOCATION

PERSON INVOLVED / INJURED   ☐ EMPLOYEE   ☐ VISITOR   ☐ OTHER / ....

FULL NAME

ADDRESS

PHONE NUMBER   E-MAIL

DESCRIPTION OF INCIDENT

....

....

....

....

....

....

ACTION TAKEN

....

....

....

....

WITNESS/ES

FULL NAME   CONTACT

FULL NAME   CONTACT

FULL NAME   CONTACT

FORM COMPLETED BY   SIGNED BY

APPROVED BY   SIGNED BY

Incident Report Log Book

INCIDENT REPORT FORM

INCIDENT DATE

REPORT DATE

INCIDENT TIME

LOCATION

PERSON INVOLVED / INJURED ☐ EMPLOYEE ☐ VISITOR ☐ OTHER / ....

FULL NAME

ADDRESS

PHONE NUMBER

E-MAIL

DESCRIPTION OF INCIDENT

....
....
....
....
....
....

ACTION TAKEN

....
....
....
....

WITNESS/ES

FULL NAME

CONTACT

FULL NAME

CONTACT

FULL NAME

CONTACT

FORM COMPLETED BY

SIGNED BY

APPROVED BY

SIGNED BY

Incident Report Log Book

INCIDENT REPORT FORM

INCIDENT DATE

REPORT DATE

INCIDENT TIME

LOCATION

PERSON INVOLVED / INJURED ☐ EMPLOYEE ☐ VISITOR ☐ OTHER / ....

FULL NAME

ADDRESS

PHONE NUMBER

E-MAIL

DESCRIPTION OF INCIDENT

....
....
....
....
....
....

ACTION TAKEN

....
....
....
....

WITNESS/ES

FULL NAME

CONTACT

FULL NAME

CONTACT

FULL NAME

CONTACT

FORM COMPLETED BY

SIGNED BY

APPROVED BY

SIGNED BY

Incident Report Log Book

INCIDENT REPORT FORM

INCIDENT DATE

INCIDENT TIME

REPORT DATE

LOCATION

PERSON INVOLVED / INJURED ☐ EMPLOYEE ☐ VISITOR ☐ OTHER / ....

FULL NAME

ADDRESS

PHONE NUMBER **E-MAIL**

DESCRIPTION OF INCIDENT

....
....
....
....
....
....

ACTION TAKEN

....
....
....
....

WITNESS/ES

FULL NAME **CONTACT**

FULL NAME **CONTACT**

FULL NAME **CONTACT**

FORM COMPLETED BY **SIGNED BY**

APPROVED BY **SIGNED BY**

Incident Report Log Book

INCIDENT REPORT FORM

INCIDENT DATE   REPORT DATE

INCIDENT TIME   LOCATION

PERSON INVOLVED / INJURED   ☐ EMPLOYEE   ☐ VISITOR   ☐ OTHER / ....

FULL NAME

ADDRESS

PHONE NUMBER   E-MAIL

DESCRIPTION OF INCIDENT

....
....
....
....
....
....

ACTION TAKEN

....
....
....
....

WITNESS/ES

FULL NAME   CONTACT

FULL NAME   CONTACT

FULL NAME   CONTACT

FORM COMPLETED BY   SIGNED BY

APPROVED BY   SIGNED BY

Incident Report Log Book

INCIDENT REPORT FORM

INCIDENT DATE

REPORT DATE

INCIDENT TIME

LOCATION

PERSON INVOLVED / INJURED ☐ **EMPLOYEE** ☐ **VISITOR** ☐ **OTHER /** ....

FULL NAME

ADDRESS

PHONE NUMBER

E-MAIL

DESCRIPTION OF INCIDENT

....
....
....
....
....
....

ACTION TAKEN

....
....
....
....

WITNESS/ES

FULL NAME

CONTACT

FULL NAME

CONTACT

FULL NAME

CONTACT

FORM COMPLETED BY

SIGNED BY

APPROVED BY

SIGNED BY

Incident Report Log Book

INCIDENT REPORT FORM

INCIDENT DATE   REPORT DATE

INCIDENT TIME   LOCATION

PERSON INVOLVED / INJURED   ☐ EMPLOYEE ☐ VISITOR ☐ OTHER / ....

FULL NAME

ADDRESS

PHONE NUMBER   E-MAIL

DESCRIPTION OF INCIDENT

....
....
....
....
....
....

ACTION TAKEN

....
....
....
....

WITNESS/ES

FULL NAME   CONTACT

FULL NAME   CONTACT

FULL NAME   CONTACT

FORM COMPLETED BY   SIGNED BY

APPROVED BY   SIGNED BY

Incident Report Log Book

INCIDENT REPORT FORM

INCIDENT DATE .... **REPORT DATE** ....

INCIDENT TIME .... **LOCATION** ....

PERSON INVOLVED / INJURED ☐ **EMPLOYEE** ☐ **VISITOR** ☐ **OTHER /** ....

FULL NAME ....

ADDRESS ....

PHONE NUMBER .... **E-MAIL** ....

DESCRIPTION OF INCIDENT

....
....
....
....
....
....

ACTION TAKEN

....
....
....
....

WITNESS/ES

FULL NAME .... **CONTACT** ....

FULL NAME .... **CONTACT** ....

FULL NAME .... **CONTACT** ....

FORM COMPLETED BY .... **SIGNED BY** ....

APPROVED BY .... **SIGNED BY** ....

Incident Report Log Book

INCIDENT REPORT FORM

INCIDENT DATE   REPORT DATE

INCIDENT TIME   LOCATION

PERSON INVOLVED / INJURED ☐ EMPLOYEE ☐ VISITOR ☐ OTHER / ....

FULL NAME

ADDRESS

PHONE NUMBER   E-MAIL

DESCRIPTION OF INCIDENT

....
....
....
....
....
....

ACTION TAKEN

....
....
....
....

WITNESS/ES

FULL NAME   CONTACT

FULL NAME   CONTACT

FULL NAME   CONTACT

FORM COMPLETED BY   SIGNED BY

APPROVED BY   SIGNED BY

Incident Report Log Book

INCIDENT REPORT FORM

INCIDENT DATE

REPORT DATE

INCIDENT TIME

LOCATION

PERSON INVOLVED / INJURED ☐ EMPLOYEE ☐ VISITOR ☐ OTHER / ....

FULL NAME

ADDRESS

PHONE NUMBER

E-MAIL

DESCRIPTION OF INCIDENT

....
....
....
....
....
....

ACTION TAKEN

....
....
....
....

WITNESS/ES

FULL NAME

CONTACT

FULL NAME

CONTACT

FULL NAME

CONTACT

FORM COMPLETED BY

SIGNED BY

APPROVED BY

SIGNED BY

Incident Report Log Book

INCIDENT REPORT FORM

INCIDENT DATE   **REPORT DATE**

INCIDENT TIME   **LOCATION**

PERSON INVOLVED / INJURED   ☐ EMPLOYEE   ☐ VISITOR   ☐ OTHER / ....

FULL NAME

ADDRESS

PHONE NUMBER   **E-MAIL**

DESCRIPTION OF INCIDENT

....
....
....
....
....
....

ACTION TAKEN

....
....
....
....

WITNESS/ES

FULL NAME   **CONTACT**

FULL NAME   **CONTACT**

FULL NAME   **CONTACT**

FORM COMPLETED BY   **SIGNED BY**

APPROVED BY   **SIGNED BY**

Incident Report Log Book

INCIDENT REPORT FORM

INCIDENT DATE

REPORT DATE

INCIDENT TIME

LOCATION

PERSON INVOLVED / INJURED ☐ **EMPLOYEE** ☐ **VISITOR** ☐ **OTHER /** ....

FULL NAME

ADDRESS

PHONE NUMBER　　　　　　　**E-MAIL**

DESCRIPTION OF INCIDENT

....
....
....
....
....
....

ACTION TAKEN

....
....
....
....

WITNESS/ES

FULL NAME　　　　　　　　　**CONTACT**

FULL NAME　　　　　　　　　**CONTACT**

FULL NAME　　　　　　　　　**CONTACT**

FORM COMPLETED BY　　　　**SIGNED BY**

APPROVED BY　　　　　　　　**SIGNED BY**

Incident Report Log Book

INCIDENT REPORT FORM

INCIDENT DATE   REPORT DATE

INCIDENT TIME   LOCATION

PERSON INVOLVED / INJURED   ☐ EMPLOYEE   ☐ VISITOR   ☐ OTHER / ....

FULL NAME

ADDRESS

PHONE NUMBER   E-MAIL

DESCRIPTION OF INCIDENT

....
....
....
....
....
....

ACTION TAKEN

....
....
....
....

WITNESS/ES

FULL NAME   CONTACT

FULL NAME   CONTACT

FULL NAME   CONTACT

FORM COMPLETED BY   SIGNED BY

APPROVED BY   SIGNED BY

Incident Report Log Book

INCIDENT REPORT FORM

INCIDENT DATE .... **REPORT DATE** ....

INCIDENT TIME .... **LOCATION** ....

PERSON INVOLVED / INJURED ☐ **EMPLOYEE** ☐ **VISITOR** ☐ **OTHER / ....**

FULL NAME

ADDRESS

PHONE NUMBER .... **E-MAIL**

DESCRIPTION OF INCIDENT

....

....

....

....

....

....

ACTION TAKEN

....

....

....

....

WITNESS/ES

FULL NAME .... **CONTACT** ....

FULL NAME .... **CONTACT** ....

FULL NAME .... **CONTACT** ....

FORM COMPLETED BY .... **SIGNED BY** ....

APPROVED BY .... **SIGNED BY** ....

Incident Report Log Book

INCIDENT REPORT FORM

INCIDENT DATE

REPORT DATE

INCIDENT TIME

LOCATION

PERSON INVOLVED / INJURED ☐ EMPLOYEE ☐ VISITOR ☐ OTHER / ....

FULL NAME

ADDRESS

PHONE NUMBER   E-MAIL

DESCRIPTION OF INCIDENT

....
....
....
....
....
....

ACTION TAKEN

....
....
....
....

WITNESS/ES

FULL NAME   CONTACT

FULL NAME   CONTACT

FULL NAME   CONTACT

FORM COMPLETED BY   SIGNED BY

APPROVED BY   SIGNED BY

Incident Report Log Book

INCIDENT REPORT FORM

INCIDENT DATE

REPORT DATE

INCIDENT TIME

LOCATION

PERSON INVOLVED / INJURED ☐ **EMPLOYEE** ☐ **VISITOR** ☐ **OTHER /** ....

FULL NAME

ADDRESS

PHONE NUMBER

E-MAIL

DESCRIPTION OF INCIDENT

....
....
....
....
....
....

ACTION TAKEN

....
....
....
....

WITNESS/ES

FULL NAME

CONTACT

FULL NAME

CONTACT

FULL NAME

CONTACT

FORM COMPLETED BY

SIGNED BY

APPROVED BY

SIGNED BY

Incident Report Log Book

INCIDENT REPORT FORM

INCIDENT DATE

REPORT DATE

INCIDENT TIME

LOCATION

PERSON INVOLVED / INJURED ☐ EMPLOYEE ☐ VISITOR ☐ OTHER / ....

FULL NAME

ADDRESS

PHONE NUMBER

E-MAIL

DESCRIPTION OF INCIDENT

....
....
....
....
....
....

ACTION TAKEN

....
....
....
....

WITNESS/ES

FULL NAME

CONTACT

FULL NAME

CONTACT

FULL NAME

CONTACT

FORM COMPLETED BY

SIGNED BY

APPROVED BY

SIGNED BY

Incident Report Log Book

INCIDENT REPORT FORM

INCIDENT DATE

REPORT DATE

INCIDENT TIME

LOCATION

PERSON INVOLVED / INJURED ☐ EMPLOYEE ☐ VISITOR ☐ OTHER / ....

FULL NAME

ADDRESS

PHONE NUMBER **E-MAIL**

DESCRIPTION OF INCIDENT

....
....
....
....
....
....

ACTION TAKEN

....
....
....
....

WITNESS/ES

FULL NAME **CONTACT**

FULL NAME **CONTACT**

FULL NAME **CONTACT**

FORM COMPLETED BY **SIGNED BY**

APPROVED BY **SIGNED BY**

Incident Report Log Book

INCIDENT REPORT FORM

INCIDENT DATE

REPORT DATE

INCIDENT TIME

LOCATION

PERSON INVOLVED / INJURED ☐ EMPLOYEE ☐ VISITOR ☐ OTHER / ....

FULL NAME

ADDRESS

PHONE NUMBER

E-MAIL

DESCRIPTION OF INCIDENT

....
....
....
....
....
....

ACTION TAKEN

....
....
....
....

WITNESS/ES

FULL NAME

CONTACT

FULL NAME

CONTACT

FULL NAME

CONTACT

FORM COMPLETED BY

SIGNED BY

APPROVED BY

SIGNED BY

Incident Report Log Book

INCIDENT REPORT FORM

INCIDENT DATE   **REPORT DATE**

INCIDENT TIME   **LOCATION**

PERSON INVOLVED / INJURED   ☐ EMPLOYEE   ☐ VISITOR   ☐ OTHER / ....

FULL NAME

ADDRESS

PHONE NUMBER   **E-MAIL**

DESCRIPTION OF INCIDENT

....
....
....
....
....
....

ACTION TAKEN

....
....
....
....

WITNESS/ES

FULL NAME   **CONTACT**

FULL NAME   **CONTACT**

FULL NAME   **CONTACT**

FORM COMPLETED BY   **SIGNED BY**

APPROVED BY   **SIGNED BY**

Incident Report Log Book

INCIDENT REPORT FORM

INCIDENT DATE   REPORT DATE

INCIDENT TIME   LOCATION

PERSON INVOLVED / INJURED   ☐ EMPLOYEE   ☐ VISITOR   ☐ OTHER / ....

FULL NAME

ADDRESS

PHONE NUMBER   E-MAIL

DESCRIPTION OF INCIDENT

....
....
....
....
....
....

ACTION TAKEN

....
....
....
....

WITNESS/ES

FULL NAME   CONTACT

FULL NAME   CONTACT

FULL NAME   CONTACT

FORM COMPLETED BY   SIGNED BY

APPROVED BY   SIGNED BY

Incident Report Log Book

INCIDENT REPORT FORM

INCIDENT DATE

REPORT DATE

INCIDENT TIME

LOCATION

PERSON INVOLVED / INJURED ☐ EMPLOYEE ☐ VISITOR ☐ OTHER / ....

FULL NAME

ADDRESS

PHONE NUMBER

E-MAIL

DESCRIPTION OF INCIDENT

....
....
....
....
....
....

ACTION TAKEN

....
....
....
....

WITNESS/ES

FULL NAME

CONTACT

FULL NAME

CONTACT

FULL NAME

CONTACT

FORM COMPLETED BY

SIGNED BY

APPROVED BY

SIGNED BY

Incident Report Log Book

INCIDENT REPORT FORM

INCIDENT DATE .... REPORT DATE ....

INCIDENT TIME .... LOCATION ....

PERSON INVOLVED / INJURED ☐ EMPLOYEE ☐ VISITOR ☐ OTHER / ....

FULL NAME ....

ADDRESS ....

PHONE NUMBER .... E-MAIL

DESCRIPTION OF INCIDENT

....
....
....
....
....
....

ACTION TAKEN

....
....
....
....

WITNESS/ES

FULL NAME .... CONTACT ....

FULL NAME .... CONTACT ....

FULL NAME .... CONTACT ....

FORM COMPLETED BY .... SIGNED BY ....

APPROVED BY .... SIGNED BY ....

Incident Report Log Book

INCIDENT REPORT FORM

INCIDENT DATE

REPORT DATE

INCIDENT TIME

LOCATION

PERSON INVOLVED / INJURED   ☐ EMPLOYEE   ☐ VISITOR   ☐ OTHER / ....

FULL NAME

ADDRESS

PHONE NUMBER   **E-MAIL**

DESCRIPTION OF INCIDENT

....
....
....
....
....
....

ACTION TAKEN

....
....
....
....

WITNESS/ES

FULL NAME   **CONTACT**

FULL NAME   **CONTACT**

FULL NAME   **CONTACT**

FORM COMPLETED BY   **SIGNED BY**

APPROVED BY   **SIGNED BY**

Incident Report Log Book

INCIDENT REPORT FORM

INCIDENT DATE   **REPORT DATE**

INCIDENT TIME   **LOCATION**

PERSON INVOLVED / INJURED   ☐ **EMPLOYEE**   ☐ **VISITOR**   ☐ **OTHER** / ....

FULL NAME

ADDRESS

PHONE NUMBER   **E-MAIL**

DESCRIPTION OF INCIDENT

....
....
....
....
....
....

ACTION TAKEN

....
....
....
....

WITNESS/ES

FULL NAME   **CONTACT**

FULL NAME   **CONTACT**

FULL NAME   **CONTACT**

FORM COMPLETED BY   **SIGNED BY**

APPROVED BY   **SIGNED BY**

Incident Report Log Book

INCIDENT REPORT FORM

INCIDENT DATE   **REPORT DATE**

INCIDENT TIME   **LOCATION**

PERSON INVOLVED / INJURED   ☐ **EMPLOYEE**   ☐ **VISITOR**   ☐ **OTHER** / ....

FULL NAME

ADDRESS

PHONE NUMBER   **E-MAIL**

DESCRIPTION OF INCIDENT

....
....
....
....
....
....

ACTION TAKEN

....
....
....
....

WITNESS/ES

FULL NAME   **CONTACT**

FULL NAME   **CONTACT**

FULL NAME   **CONTACT**

FORM COMPLETED BY   **SIGNED BY**

APPROVED BY   **SIGNED BY**

Incident Report Log Book

INCIDENT REPORT FORM

INCIDENT DATE

REPORT DATE

INCIDENT TIME

LOCATION

PERSON INVOLVED / INJURED ☐ EMPLOYEE ☐ VISITOR ☐ OTHER / ....

FULL NAME

ADDRESS

PHONE NUMBER

E-MAIL

DESCRIPTION OF INCIDENT

....
....
....
....
....
....

ACTION TAKEN

....
....
....
....

WITNESS/ES

FULL NAME

CONTACT

FULL NAME

CONTACT

FULL NAME

CONTACT

FORM COMPLETED BY

SIGNED BY

APPROVED BY

SIGNED BY

Incident Report Log Book

INCIDENT REPORT FORM

INCIDENT DATE

REPORT DATE

INCIDENT TIME

LOCATION

PERSON INVOLVED / INJURED ☐ **EMPLOYEE** ☐ **VISITOR** ☐ **OTHER /** ....

FULL NAME

ADDRESS

PHONE NUMBER **E-MAIL**

DESCRIPTION OF INCIDENT

....
....
....
....
....
....

ACTION TAKEN

....
....
....
....

WITNESS/ES

FULL NAME **CONTACT**

FULL NAME **CONTACT**

FULL NAME **CONTACT**

FORM COMPLETED BY **SIGNED BY**

APPROVED BY **SIGNED BY**

Incident Report Log Book

INCIDENT REPORT FORM

INCIDENT DATE

INCIDENT TIME

PERSON INVOLVED / INJURED   ☐ EMPLOYEE   ☐ VISITOR   ☐ OTHER / ....

FULL NAME

ADDRESS

PHONE NUMBER

REPORT DATE

LOCATION

E-MAIL

DESCRIPTION OF INCIDENT

....
....
....
....
....
....

ACTION TAKEN

....
....
....
....

WITNESS/ES

FULL NAME   **CONTACT**

FULL NAME   **CONTACT**

FULL NAME   **CONTACT**

FORM COMPLETED BY   **SIGNED BY**

APPROVED BY   **SIGNED BY**

Incident Report Log Book

INCIDENT REPORT FORM

INCIDENT DATE

INCIDENT TIME

REPORT DATE

LOCATION

PERSON INVOLVED / INJURED ☐ **EMPLOYEE** ☐ **VISITOR** ☐ **OTHER /** ....

FULL NAME

ADDRESS

PHONE NUMBER   **E-MAIL**

DESCRIPTION OF INCIDENT

....
....
....
....
....
....

ACTION TAKEN

....
....
....
....

WITNESS/ES

FULL NAME   **CONTACT**

FULL NAME   **CONTACT**

FULL NAME   **CONTACT**

FORM COMPLETED BY   **SIGNED BY**

APPROVED BY   **SIGNED BY**

Incident Report Log Book

INCIDENT REPORT FORM

INCIDENT DATE   **REPORT DATE**

INCIDENT TIME   **LOCATION**

PERSON INVOLVED / INJURED   ☐ **EMPLOYEE**   ☐ **VISITOR**   ☐ **OTHER /** ....

FULL NAME

ADDRESS

PHONE NUMBER   **E-MAIL**

DESCRIPTION OF INCIDENT

....
....
....
....
....
....

ACTION TAKEN

....
....
....
....

WITNESS/ES

FULL NAME   **CONTACT**

FULL NAME   **CONTACT**

FULL NAME   **CONTACT**

FORM COMPLETED BY   **SIGNED BY**

APPROVED BY   **SIGNED BY**

Incident Report Log Book

INCIDENT REPORT FORM

INCIDENT DATE

REPORT DATE

INCIDENT TIME

LOCATION

PERSON INVOLVED / INJURED ☐ EMPLOYEE ☐ VISITOR ☐ OTHER / ....

FULL NAME

ADDRESS

PHONE NUMBER

E-MAIL

DESCRIPTION OF INCIDENT

....
....
....
....
....
....

ACTION TAKEN

....
....
....
....

WITNESS/ES

FULL NAME

CONTACT

FULL NAME

CONTACT

FULL NAME

CONTACT

FORM COMPLETED BY

SIGNED BY

APPROVED BY

SIGNED BY

Incident Report Log Book

INCIDENT REPORT FORM

INCIDENT DATE

REPORT DATE

INCIDENT TIME

LOCATION

PERSON INVOLVED / INJURED ☐ EMPLOYEE ☐ VISITOR ☐ OTHER / ....

FULL NAME

ADDRESS

PHONE NUMBER

E-MAIL

DESCRIPTION OF INCIDENT

....
....
....
....
....
....

ACTION TAKEN

....
....
....
....

WITNESS/ES

FULL NAME

CONTACT

FULL NAME

CONTACT

FULL NAME

CONTACT

FORM COMPLETED BY

SIGNED BY

APPROVED BY

SIGNED BY

Incident Report Log Book

INCIDENT REPORT FORM

INCIDENT DATE

REPORT DATE

INCIDENT TIME

LOCATION

PERSON INVOLVED / INJURED ☐ EMPLOYEE ☐ VISITOR ☐ OTHER / ....

FULL NAME

ADDRESS

PHONE NUMBER

E-MAIL

DESCRIPTION OF INCIDENT

....
....
....
....
....
....

ACTION TAKEN

....
....
....
....

WITNESS/ES

FULL NAME

CONTACT

FULL NAME

CONTACT

FULL NAME

CONTACT

FORM COMPLETED BY

SIGNED BY

APPROVED BY

SIGNED BY

Incident Report Log Book

INCIDENT REPORT FORM

INCIDENT DATE .... REPORT DATE ....

INCIDENT TIME .... LOCATION ....

PERSON INVOLVED / INJURED ☐ EMPLOYEE ☐ VISITOR ☐ OTHER / ....

FULL NAME ....

ADDRESS ....

PHONE NUMBER .... E-MAIL ....

DESCRIPTION OF INCIDENT

....
....
....
....
....
....

ACTION TAKEN

....
....
....
....

WITNESS/ES

FULL NAME .... CONTACT ....

FULL NAME .... CONTACT ....

FULL NAME .... CONTACT ....

FORM COMPLETED BY .... SIGNED BY ....

APPROVED BY .... SIGNED BY ....

Incident Report Log Book

INCIDENT REPORT FORM

INCIDENT DATE

REPORT DATE

INCIDENT TIME

LOCATION

PERSON INVOLVED / INJURED ☐ EMPLOYEE ☐ VISITOR ☐ OTHER / ....

FULL NAME

ADDRESS

PHONE NUMBER   E-MAIL

DESCRIPTION OF INCIDENT

....
....
....
....
....
....

ACTION TAKEN

....
....
....
....

WITNESS/ES

FULL NAME   CONTACT

FULL NAME   CONTACT

FULL NAME   CONTACT

FORM COMPLETED BY   SIGNED BY

APPROVED BY   SIGNED BY

Incident Report Log Book

INCIDENT REPORT FORM

INCIDENT DATE

REPORT DATE

INCIDENT TIME

LOCATION

PERSON INVOLVED / INJURED ☐ EMPLOYEE ☐ VISITOR ☐ OTHER / ....

FULL NAME

ADDRESS

PHONE NUMBER

E-MAIL

DESCRIPTION OF INCIDENT

....
....
....
....
....
....

ACTION TAKEN

....
....
....
....

WITNESS/ES

FULL NAME

CONTACT

FULL NAME

CONTACT

FULL NAME

CONTACT

FORM COMPLETED BY

SIGNED BY

APPROVED BY

SIGNED BY

Incident Report Log Book

INCIDENT REPORT FORM

INCIDENT DATE

REPORT DATE

INCIDENT TIME

LOCATION

PERSON INVOLVED / INJURED ☐ EMPLOYEE ☐ VISITOR ☐ OTHER / ....

FULL NAME

ADDRESS

PHONE NUMBER

E-MAIL

DESCRIPTION OF INCIDENT

....
....
....
....
....
....

ACTION TAKEN

....
....
....
....

WITNESS/ES

FULL NAME

CONTACT

FULL NAME

CONTACT

FULL NAME

CONTACT

FORM COMPLETED BY

SIGNED BY

APPROVED BY

SIGNED BY

Incident Report Log Book

INCIDENT REPORT FORM

INCIDENT DATE _____ REPORT DATE _____

INCIDENT TIME _____ LOCATION _____

PERSON INVOLVED / INJURED ☐ EMPLOYEE ☐ VISITOR ☐ OTHER / ....

FULL NAME _____

ADDRESS _____

PHONE NUMBER _____ E-MAIL _____

DESCRIPTION OF INCIDENT

....
....
....
....
....
....

ACTION TAKEN

....
....
....
....

WITNESS/ES

FULL NAME _____ CONTACT _____

FULL NAME _____ CONTACT _____

FULL NAME _____ CONTACT _____

FORM COMPLETED BY _____ SIGNED BY _____

APPROVED BY _____ SIGNED BY _____

Incident Report Log Book

INCIDENT REPORT FORM

INCIDENT DATE

REPORT DATE

INCIDENT TIME

LOCATION

PERSON INVOLVED / INJURED ☐ EMPLOYEE ☐ VISITOR ☐ OTHER / ....

FULL NAME

ADDRESS

PHONE NUMBER   **E-MAIL**

DESCRIPTION OF INCIDENT

ACTION TAKEN

WITNESS/ES

FULL NAME   **CONTACT**

FULL NAME   **CONTACT**

FULL NAME   **CONTACT**

FORM COMPLETED BY   **SIGNED BY**

APPROVED BY   **SIGNED BY**

Incident Report Log Book

INCIDENT REPORT FORM

INCIDENT DATE

REPORT DATE

INCIDENT TIME

LOCATION

PERSON INVOLVED / INJURED ☐ EMPLOYEE ☐ VISITOR ☐ OTHER / ....

FULL NAME

ADDRESS

PHONE NUMBER

E-MAIL

DESCRIPTION OF INCIDENT

....
....
....
....
....
....

ACTION TAKEN

....
....
....
....

WITNESS/ES

FULL NAME

CONTACT

FULL NAME

CONTACT

FULL NAME

CONTACT

FORM COMPLETED BY

SIGNED BY

APPROVED BY

SIGNED BY

Incident Report Log Book

INCIDENT REPORT FORM

INCIDENT DATE

REPORT DATE

INCIDENT TIME

LOCATION

PERSON INVOLVED / INJURED ☐ EMPLOYEE ☐ VISITOR ☐ OTHER / ....

FULL NAME

ADDRESS

PHONE NUMBER

E-MAIL

DESCRIPTION OF INCIDENT

....
....
....
....
....
....

ACTION TAKEN

....
....
....
....

WITNESS/ES

FULL NAME

CONTACT

FULL NAME

CONTACT

FULL NAME

CONTACT

FORM COMPLETED BY

SIGNED BY

APPROVED BY

SIGNED BY

Incident Report Log Book

INCIDENT REPORT FORM

INCIDENT DATE _____   **REPORT DATE** _____

INCIDENT TIME _____   **LOCATION** _____

PERSON INVOLVED / INJURED   ☐ EMPLOYEE   ☐ VISITOR   ☐ OTHER / ....

FULL NAME _____

ADDRESS _____

PHONE NUMBER _____   **E-MAIL** _____

DESCRIPTION OF INCIDENT

....
....
....
....
....
....

ACTION TAKEN

....
....
....
....

WITNESS/ES

FULL NAME _____   **CONTACT** _____

FULL NAME _____   **CONTACT** _____

FULL NAME _____   **CONTACT** _____

FORM COMPLETED BY _____   **SIGNED BY** _____

APPROVED BY _____   **SIGNED BY** _____

Incident Report Log Book

INCIDENT REPORT FORM

INCIDENT DATE

INCIDENT TIME

PERSON INVOLVED / INJURED ☐ **EMPLOYEE** ☐ **VISITOR** ☐ **OTHER /** ....

FULL NAME

ADDRESS

PHONE NUMBER

REPORT DATE

LOCATION

E-MAIL

DESCRIPTION OF INCIDENT

....
....
....
....
....
....

ACTION TAKEN

....
....
....
....

WITNESS/ES

FULL NAME **CONTACT**

FULL NAME **CONTACT**

FULL NAME **CONTACT**

FORM COMPLETED BY **SIGNED BY**

APPROVED BY **SIGNED BY**

Incident Report Log Book

INCIDENT REPORT FORM

INCIDENT DATE

REPORT DATE

INCIDENT TIME

LOCATION

PERSON INVOLVED / INJURED ☐ EMPLOYEE ☐ VISITOR ☐ OTHER / ....

FULL NAME

ADDRESS

PHONE NUMBER

E-MAIL

DESCRIPTION OF INCIDENT

....

....

....

....

....

....

ACTION TAKEN

....

....

....

....

WITNESS/ES

FULL NAME

CONTACT

FULL NAME

CONTACT

FULL NAME

CONTACT

FORM COMPLETED BY

SIGNED BY

APPROVED BY

SIGNED BY

Incident Report Log Book

INCIDENT REPORT FORM

INCIDENT DATE   REPORT DATE

INCIDENT TIME   LOCATION

PERSON INVOLVED / INJURED   ☐ EMPLOYEE   ☐ VISITOR   ☐ OTHER / ....

FULL NAME

ADDRESS

PHONE NUMBER   E-MAIL

DESCRIPTION OF INCIDENT

....
....
....
....
....
....

ACTION TAKEN

....
....
....
....

WITNESS/ES

FULL NAME   CONTACT

FULL NAME   CONTACT

FULL NAME   CONTACT

FORM COMPLETED BY   SIGNED BY

APPROVED BY   SIGNED BY

Incident Report Log Book

INCIDENT REPORT FORM

INCIDENT DATE

REPORT DATE

INCIDENT TIME

LOCATION

PERSON INVOLVED / INJURED ☐ **EMPLOYEE** ☐ **VISITOR** ☐ **OTHER /** ....

FULL NAME

ADDRESS

PHONE NUMBER

E-MAIL

DESCRIPTION OF INCIDENT

....
....
....
....
....
....

ACTION TAKEN

....
....
....
....

WITNESS/ES

FULL NAME

CONTACT

FULL NAME

CONTACT

FULL NAME

CONTACT

FORM COMPLETED BY

SIGNED BY

APPROVED BY

SIGNED BY

Incident Report Log Book

INCIDENT REPORT FORM

INCIDENT DATE   **REPORT DATE**

INCIDENT TIME   **LOCATION**

PERSON INVOLVED / INJURED   ☐ **EMPLOYEE**   ☐ **VISITOR**   ☐ **OTHER /** ....

FULL NAME

ADDRESS

PHONE NUMBER   **E-MAIL**

DESCRIPTION OF INCIDENT

....
....
....
....
....
....

ACTION TAKEN

....
....
....
....

WITNESS/ES

FULL NAME   **CONTACT**

FULL NAME   **CONTACT**

FULL NAME   **CONTACT**

FORM COMPLETED BY   **SIGNED BY**

APPROVED BY   **SIGNED BY**

Incident Report Log Book

INCIDENT REPORT FORM

INCIDENT DATE

REPORT DATE

INCIDENT TIME

LOCATION

PERSON INVOLVED / INJURED   ☐ **EMPLOYEE**   ☐ **VISITOR**   ☐ **OTHER / ....**

FULL NAME

ADDRESS

PHONE NUMBER   **E-MAIL**

DESCRIPTION OF INCIDENT

....
....
....
....
....
....

ACTION TAKEN

....
....
....
....

WITNESS/ES

FULL NAME   **CONTACT**

FULL NAME   **CONTACT**

FULL NAME   **CONTACT**

FORM COMPLETED BY   **SIGNED BY**

APPROVED BY   **SIGNED BY**

Incident Report Log Book

INCIDENT REPORT FORM

INCIDENT DATE

REPORT DATE

INCIDENT TIME

LOCATION

PERSON INVOLVED / INJURED ☐ EMPLOYEE ☐ VISITOR ☐ OTHER / ....

FULL NAME

ADDRESS

PHONE NUMBER

E-MAIL

DESCRIPTION OF INCIDENT

....
....
....
....
....
....

ACTION TAKEN

....
....
....
....

WITNESS/ES

FULL NAME

CONTACT

FULL NAME

CONTACT

FULL NAME

CONTACT

FORM COMPLETED BY

SIGNED BY

APPROVED BY

SIGNED BY

Incident Report Log Book

INCIDENT REPORT FORM

INCIDENT DATE

INCIDENT TIME

PERSON INVOLVED / INJURED   ☐ EMPLOYEE   ☐ VISITOR   ☐ OTHER / ....

FULL NAME

ADDRESS

PHONE NUMBER

REPORT DATE

LOCATION

E-MAIL

DESCRIPTION OF INCIDENT

....
....
....
....
....
....

ACTION TAKEN

....
....
....
....

WITNESS/ES

FULL NAME   **CONTACT**

FULL NAME   **CONTACT**

FULL NAME   **CONTACT**

FORM COMPLETED BY   **SIGNED BY**

APPROVED BY   **SIGNED BY**

Incident Report Log Book

INCIDENT REPORT FORM

INCIDENT DATE

INCIDENT TIME

REPORT DATE

LOCATION

PERSON INVOLVED / INJURED ☐ **EMPLOYEE** ☐ **VISITOR** ☐ **OTHER /** ....

FULL NAME

ADDRESS

PHONE NUMBER   **E-MAIL**

DESCRIPTION OF INCIDENT

....

....

....

....

....

....

ACTION TAKEN

....

....

....

....

WITNESS/ES

FULL NAME   **CONTACT**

FULL NAME   **CONTACT**

FULL NAME   **CONTACT**

FORM COMPLETED BY   **SIGNED BY**

APPROVED BY   **SIGNED BY**

Incident Report Log Book

INCIDENT REPORT FORM

INCIDENT DATE .... **REPORT DATE** ....

INCIDENT TIME .... **LOCATION** ....

PERSON INVOLVED / INJURED ☐ EMPLOYEE ☐ VISITOR ☐ OTHER / ....

FULL NAME ....

ADDRESS ....

PHONE NUMBER .... **E-MAIL** ....

DESCRIPTION OF INCIDENT

....
....
....
....
....
....

ACTION TAKEN

....
....
....
....

WITNESS/ES

FULL NAME .... **CONTACT** ....

FULL NAME .... **CONTACT** ....

FULL NAME .... **CONTACT** ....

FORM COMPLETED BY .... **SIGNED BY** ....

APPROVED BY .... **SIGNED BY** ....

Incident Report Log Book

INCIDENT REPORT FORM

INCIDENT DATE

REPORT DATE

INCIDENT TIME

LOCATION

PERSON INVOLVED / INJURED ☐ EMPLOYEE ☐ VISITOR ☐ OTHER / ....

FULL NAME

ADDRESS

PHONE NUMBER

E-MAIL

DESCRIPTION OF INCIDENT

....
....
....
....
....
....

ACTION TAKEN

....
....
....
....

WITNESS/ES

FULL NAME

CONTACT

FULL NAME

CONTACT

FULL NAME

CONTACT

FORM COMPLETED BY

SIGNED BY

APPROVED BY

SIGNED BY

Incident Report Log Book

INCIDENT REPORT FORM

INCIDENT DATE   REPORT DATE

INCIDENT TIME   LOCATION

PERSON INVOLVED / INJURED   ☐ EMPLOYEE   ☐ VISITOR   ☐ OTHER / ....

FULL NAME

ADDRESS

PHONE NUMBER   E-MAIL

DESCRIPTION OF INCIDENT

....
....
....
....
....
....

ACTION TAKEN

....
....
....
....

WITNESS/ES

FULL NAME   CONTACT

FULL NAME   CONTACT

FULL NAME   CONTACT

FORM COMPLETED BY   SIGNED BY

APPROVED BY   SIGNED BY

Incident Report Log Book

INCIDENT REPORT FORM

INCIDENT DATE

REPORT DATE

INCIDENT TIME

LOCATION

PERSON INVOLVED / INJURED ☐ EMPLOYEE ☐ VISITOR ☐ OTHER / ....

FULL NAME

ADDRESS

PHONE NUMBER

E-MAIL

DESCRIPTION OF INCIDENT

....
....
....
....
....
....

ACTION TAKEN

....
....
....
....

WITNESS/ES

FULL NAME

CONTACT

FULL NAME

CONTACT

FULL NAME

CONTACT

FORM COMPLETED BY

SIGNED BY

APPROVED BY

SIGNED BY

Incident Report Log Book

INCIDENT REPORT FORM

INCIDENT DATE		**REPORT DATE**
INCIDENT TIME		**LOCATION**

PERSON INVOLVED / INJURED ☐ **EMPLOYEE** ☐ **VISITOR** ☐ **OTHER / ....**

FULL NAME

ADDRESS

PHONE NUMBER **E-MAIL**

DESCRIPTION OF INCIDENT

....
....
....
....
....
....

ACTION TAKEN

....
....
....
....

WITNESS/ES

FULL NAME	**CONTACT**
FULL NAME	**CONTACT**
FULL NAME	**CONTACT**
FORM COMPLETED BY	**SIGNED BY**
APPROVED BY	**SIGNED BY**

Incident Report Log Book

INCIDENT REPORT FORM

INCIDENT DATE   REPORT DATE

INCIDENT TIME   LOCATION

PERSON INVOLVED / INJURED   ☐ EMPLOYEE   ☐ VISITOR   ☐ OTHER / ....

FULL NAME

ADDRESS

PHONE NUMBER   E-MAIL

DESCRIPTION OF INCIDENT

....
....
....
....
....
....

ACTION TAKEN

....
....
....
....

WITNESS/ES

FULL NAME   CONTACT

FULL NAME   CONTACT

FULL NAME   CONTACT

FORM COMPLETED BY   SIGNED BY

APPROVED BY   SIGNED BY

Incident Report Log Book

INCIDENT REPORT FORM

INCIDENT DATE

REPORT DATE

INCIDENT TIME

LOCATION

PERSON INVOLVED / INJURED ☐ **EMPLOYEE** ☐ **VISITOR** ☐ **OTHER /** ....

FULL NAME

ADDRESS

PHONE NUMBER

E-MAIL

DESCRIPTION OF INCIDENT

....
....
....
....
....
....

ACTION TAKEN

....
....
....
....

WITNESS/ES

FULL NAME

CONTACT

FULL NAME

CONTACT

FULL NAME

CONTACT

FORM COMPLETED BY

SIGNED BY

APPROVED BY

SIGNED BY

Incident Report Log Book

INCIDENT REPORT FORM

INCIDENT DATE

REPORT DATE

INCIDENT TIME

LOCATION

PERSON INVOLVED / INJURED ☐ EMPLOYEE ☐ VISITOR ☐ OTHER / ....

FULL NAME

ADDRESS

PHONE NUMBER   E-MAIL

DESCRIPTION OF INCIDENT

....
....
....
....
....
....

ACTION TAKEN

....
....
....
....

WITNESS/ES

FULL NAME   CONTACT

FULL NAME   CONTACT

FULL NAME   CONTACT

FORM COMPLETED BY   SIGNED BY

APPROVED BY   SIGNED BY

Incident Report Log Book

INCIDENT REPORT FORM

INCIDENT DATE   **REPORT DATE**

INCIDENT TIME   **LOCATION**

PERSON INVOLVED / INJURED   ☐ **EMPLOYEE**   ☐ **VISITOR**   ☐ **OTHER /** ....

FULL NAME

ADDRESS

PHONE NUMBER   **E-MAIL**

DESCRIPTION OF INCIDENT

....
....
....
....
....
....

ACTION TAKEN

....
....
....
....

WITNESS/ES

FULL NAME   **CONTACT**

FULL NAME   **CONTACT**

FULL NAME   **CONTACT**

FORM COMPLETED BY   **SIGNED BY**

APPROVED BY   **SIGNED BY**

Incident Report Log Book

INCIDENT REPORT FORM

INCIDENT DATE

REPORT DATE

INCIDENT TIME

LOCATION

PERSON INVOLVED / INJURED ☐ EMPLOYEE ☐ VISITOR ☐ OTHER / ....

FULL NAME

ADDRESS

PHONE NUMBER

E-MAIL

DESCRIPTION OF INCIDENT

....
....
....
....
....
....

ACTION TAKEN

....
....
....
....

WITNESS/ES

FULL NAME

CONTACT

FULL NAME

CONTACT

FULL NAME

CONTACT

FORM COMPLETED BY

SIGNED BY

APPROVED BY

SIGNED BY

Incident Report Log Book

INCIDENT REPORT FORM

INCIDENT DATE

REPORT DATE

INCIDENT TIME

LOCATION

PERSON INVOLVED / INJURED ☐ EMPLOYEE ☐ VISITOR ☐ OTHER / ....

FULL NAME

ADDRESS

PHONE NUMBER

E-MAIL

DESCRIPTION OF INCIDENT

....
....
....
....
....
....

ACTION TAKEN

....
....
....
....

WITNESS/ES

FULL NAME

CONTACT

FULL NAME

CONTACT

FULL NAME

CONTACT

FORM COMPLETED BY

SIGNED BY

APPROVED BY

SIGNED BY

Incident Report Log Book

INCIDENT REPORT FORM

INCIDENT DATE

REPORT DATE

INCIDENT TIME

LOCATION

PERSON INVOLVED / INJURED ☐ **EMPLOYEE** ☐ **VISITOR** ☐ **OTHER / ....**

FULL NAME

ADDRESS

PHONE NUMBER

E-MAIL

DESCRIPTION OF INCIDENT

....

....

....

....

....

....

ACTION TAKEN

....

....

....

....

WITNESS/ES

FULL NAME

CONTACT

FULL NAME

CONTACT

FULL NAME

CONTACT

FORM COMPLETED BY

SIGNED BY

APPROVED BY

SIGNED BY

Incident Report Log Book

INCIDENT REPORT FORM

INCIDENT DATE

REPORT DATE

INCIDENT TIME

LOCATION

PERSON INVOLVED / INJURED   ☐ EMPLOYEE   ☐ VISITOR   ☐ OTHER / ....

FULL NAME

ADDRESS

PHONE NUMBER

E-MAIL

DESCRIPTION OF INCIDENT

....
....
....
....
....
....

ACTION TAKEN

....
....
....
....

WITNESS/ES

FULL NAME

CONTACT

FULL NAME

CONTACT

FULL NAME

CONTACT

FORM COMPLETED BY

SIGNED BY

APPROVED BY

SIGNED BY

Incident Report Log Book

INCIDENT REPORT FORM

INCIDENT DATE

REPORT DATE

INCIDENT TIME

LOCATION

PERSON INVOLVED / INJURED   ☐ EMPLOYEE   ☐ VISITOR   ☐ OTHER / ....

FULL NAME

ADDRESS

PHONE NUMBER

E-MAIL

DESCRIPTION OF INCIDENT

....
....
....
....
....
....

ACTION TAKEN

....
....
....
....

WITNESS/ES

FULL NAME

CONTACT

FULL NAME

CONTACT

FULL NAME

CONTACT

FORM COMPLETED BY

SIGNED BY

APPROVED BY

SIGNED BY

Incident Report Log Book

INCIDENT REPORT FORM

INCIDENT DATE   REPORT DATE

INCIDENT TIME   LOCATION

PERSON INVOLVED / INJURED   ☐ EMPLOYEE   ☐ VISITOR   ☐ OTHER / ....

FULL NAME

ADDRESS

PHONE NUMBER   E-MAIL

DESCRIPTION OF INCIDENT

....
....
....
....
....
....

ACTION TAKEN

....
....
....
....

WITNESS/ES

FULL NAME   CONTACT

FULL NAME   CONTACT

FULL NAME   CONTACT

FORM COMPLETED BY   SIGNED BY

APPROVED BY   SIGNED BY

Incident Report Log Book

INCIDENT REPORT FORM

INCIDENT DATE

REPORT DATE

INCIDENT TIME

LOCATION

PERSON INVOLVED / INJURED ☐ **EMPLOYEE** ☐ **VISITOR** ☐ **OTHER /** ....

FULL NAME

ADDRESS

PHONE NUMBER

E-MAIL

DESCRIPTION OF INCIDENT

....
....
....
....
....
....

ACTION TAKEN

....
....
....
....

WITNESS/ES

FULL NAME

CONTACT

FULL NAME

CONTACT

FULL NAME

CONTACT

FORM COMPLETED BY

SIGNED BY

APPROVED BY

SIGNED BY

Printed in Great Britain
by Amazon